Weekday mornings can be rushed, but with a little prep the night before, you can save your time and grab your tasty fithess breakfast out of your fridge.
Overnight oats are a nourishing part of your breakfast - a portable, grab-and-go solution for when you're in a hurry. No need to whip something together when you wake up, they'll be ready when you are!
High in protein and fiber, this whole-grain recipe will keep hunger at bay all morning long. Even better, this recipe supports healthy digestion and can even help you beat belly bloat.

- Lemon & Honey Oats
- Vanilla & Blueberry Oats
- Banana & Vanilla Oats
- Pomegranate & Chocolate Oats
- Chocolate & Gingerbread Oats
- Peanut Butter & Jelly Oats
- Mandarin & Coconut Oats
- Bacon and Walnut Oats
- Latte & Almond Oats
- Almond & Coconut Oats
- Apple & Cinnamon Oats
- Cherry & Lavender Oats
- Pineapple & Coconut Oats
- Pumpkin & Honey Oats
- Figs & Nut Oats
- Chocolate & Banana Oats
- Raspberry & Almond Oats
- Pecans & Cocoa Oats
- Peanut Butter & Banana Oats
- Peach and Nut Oats
- Chocolate & Chia Oats
- Walnut & Vanilla Oats
- Banana & Cinnamon Oats
- Blueberry & Nut Oats
- Pineapple & Vanilla Oats
- Blueberry & Lemon Oats
- Grape & Lemon Oats
- Lime & Coconut Oats

Lemon & Honey Oats

Ingredients:

1/2 cup rolled oats
1 teaspoon lemon zest
1 teaspoon lemon juice
1/4 teaspoon vanilla extract
1/2 cup Greek-style yogurt
1/3 cup milk
2 - 3 sprigs of fresh thyme
1 teaspoon honey
Extra honey, to serve

Directions:

1. In a bowl or container, mix together the oats, lemon zest, lemon juice, vanilla extract, yogurt and milk. Remove the thyme leaves from the stems, and mix the leaves into the oatmeal along with the honey.
2. Cover the bowl with plastic wrap (or put the lid on the container) and leave in the fridge overnight.
3. In the morning, transfer the overnight oatmeal into a prettier dish if desired. Drizzle over some extra honey and enjoy!

Vanilla & Blueberry Oats

Ingredients:
1/2 cup old fashioned oats
1/2 cup vanilla almond milk
6 ounces blueberry greek yogurt
1-2 drops vanilla extract
1 tablespoon dry vanilla pudding mix
1/2 teaspoon cinnamon
1/3 cup flake cereal of choice
fresh or frozen blueberries

Directions:

1. Combine oats, milk, yogurt, vanilla, pudding mix, and cinnamon to a mason jar or other sealable container.
2. Stir contents until well mixed.
3. Top with fresh blueberries and flake cereal if desired.
4. Cover and refrigerate 4 hours or overnight.

Banana & Vanilla Oats

Ingredients:

1 large ripe/spotty banana, mashed
2 tablespoons chia seeds
1/4 teaspoon cinnamon
1/2 cup rolled oats
3/4 cup almond milk
1/4 teaspoon pure vanilla extract

Directions:

1. In a small bowl, mash the banana until almost smooth. Now stir in the chia seeds and cinnamon until combined.
2. Stir in the oats, almond milk, and vanilla. Cover and refrigerate overnight, or a minimum of 2 hours.
3. In the morning, stir the oat mixture to combine. If your Overnight Oats have a runny consistency even after they soak, simply stir in an additional 1 tablespoon chia seeds and place the mixture back in the fridge until it has thickened up. If the oat mixture is too thick, simply add a splash of milk and stir to combine.

Pomegranate & Chocolate Oats

Ingredients:

1/2 cup old-fashioned or rolled oats
1/2 cup vanilla almond milk
1/2 cup pomegranate seeds
1 tablespoon ground flax seeds
1 tablespoon cocoa nibs or coarsely chopped dark chocolate

Directions:
1. Stir together ingredients in a resealable container.
2. Cover and refrigerate overnight.
3. Stir again before serving; add additional milk for a thinner consistency.

*If you use unsweetened milk, you may want to add your sweetener of choice to taste.

Chocolate & Gingerbread Oats

Ingredients:

2 cups rolled oats
2 cups almond milk
1/4 cup chia seeds
1/2 teaspoon cinnamon
1/4 teaspoon ginger
1 teaspoon pure vanilla extract
2 teaspoons 100% pure maple syrup
2 packets or scoops of ALOHA Chocolate protein powder
Cacao nibs for topping

Directions:

1. Place all of the ingredients except for cacao nibs in a small bowl or jar.
2. Stir well and cover.
3. Place in the refrigerator overnight.
4. Top with cacao nibs.

Peanut Butter & Jelly Oats

Ingredients:

1 cup fresh or frozen strawberries
2 tsp chia seeds
2 cups old fashioned oats
2 1/2 tablespoons chia seeds
2 cups vanilla almond milk
1/2 cup plain Greek yogurt
1/4 heaping cup peanut butter
1 teaspoon vanilla extract
1/4 teaspoon sea salt

Directions:

1. Add strawberries and 2 teaspoons chia seeds to a small microwavable bowl. Microwave for 1 minute. Mash with a fork then set aside. Mix all remaining ingredients in a large bowl until well combined.
2. Add strawberry chia sauce and oatmeal mixture in alternate layers in four glasses, cover with plastic wrap, and refrigerate overnight.
3. Remove plastic wrap and serve immediately.

Mandarin & Coconut Oats

Ingredients:

2 cups rolled oats
1.5 cups milk
0.5 cups plain yogurt
1 tablespoon desiccated coconut
1/2 teaspoons vanilla extract
zest and juice of 1 clementine or mandarin

Directions:

1. Mix all the ingredients together in a bowl or jar and place in the fridge overnight or for at least 1 hour.
2. When you are ready to tuck in, remove from the fridge and top the oats with any toppings of your choice.
3. The oats can be eaten cold or warmed in the microwave for 30 – 60 seconds.

Bacon & Walnut Oats

Ingredients:

1 cup old fashioned oats
1 cup milk
2 tablespoons walnuts, chopped
2 tablespoons pure maple syrup
1/8 teaspoon ground cinnamon
1 slice maple bacon, cooked and crumbled

Directions:

1. In a pint jar or bowl, mix together the oatmeal, milk, walnuts, 1 tablespoon of the maple syrup, and the cinnamon.
2. Cover and refrigerate overnight, or for at least 5 hours.
3. Remove from the refrigerator and top with the crumbled bacon and remaining tablespoon of maple syrup.
4. These oats are good cold, room temperature or heated in the microwave.

Latte & Almond Oats

Ingredients:

1 cup rolled oats
1/4 cup coconut water
1/4 cup brewed coffee
1/4 cup almond milk
1 tablespoon maple syrup or honey
1 tablespoon coconut cream
dash of cinnamon

Directions:

1. Place all ingredients in a medium size tupperware and mix.
2. Then, transfer the tupperware into the fridge for 2 hours or overnight.
3. The next morning, add a few more tablespoons of almond milk.
4. Top with more coconut cream, shredded coconut, and cinnamon.

Almond & Coconut Oats

Ingredients:

1/2 cup rolled oats
3/4 almond milk
1 Tbsp maple syrup
1/2 tablespoon ground flaxseed
2 tablespoons shredded coconut
1/2 tablespoon mini chocolate chips

Directions:

1. Combine all ingredients in a glass jar.
2. Stir until well combined.
3. Refrigerate overnight, and enjoy cold
4. Top with chocolate chips

Apple & Cinnamon Oats

Ingredients:

1/2 cup rolled oats
1 tablespoon chia seeds
1/2 teaspoon ground cinnamon
1 medium apple, peeled and cored
2 Medjool dates, pitted
1 cup vanilla almond milk

Directions:

1. The night before, add all the ingredients to the bowl of your blender and give it a stir to ensure that everything is well combined.
2. Cover and place in the fridge for at least 3 hours, preferably overnight.
3. The next morning, blend until a smooth and creamy consistency is reached, adding more milk if the smoothie is too thick.
4. Transfer back to a bowl or glass, add desired toppings, and enjoy!

Cherry & Lavender Oats

Ingredients:
1 cup cashews
2 1/2 cups water
1/2 teaspoon dried culinary lavender
1 tablespoon sugar
1 teaspoon fresh lemon juice
1 teaspoon pure vanilla extract
1 cup rolled oats
1 cup fresh cherries, pitted and halved
2 tablespoons sliced almonds
yogurt or milk, for serving

Directions:
1. Place cashews and water in a high-powered blender and puree until very creamy and smooth. Depending on the strength of your blender, this may take up to 5 minutes.
2. Add in the lavender, sugar, lemon juice, vanilla extract and a small pinch of salt. Pulse to combine, then strain using a mesh strainer or nut-milk bag.
3. Place the cashew-lavender milk in a bowl and stir in the oats. Cover and place in the fridge and let soak 4-6 hours or overnight.
4. To serve, spoon oats into two bowls and add cherries and almonds. Enjoy!

Pineapple & Coconut Oats

Ingredients:
3/4 cup pistachios, shells removed and coarsely chopped
1/3 cup flaked coconut
1 cup rolled oats
1/2 cup chopped dried pineapple
1/4 cup wheat bran
2 tablespoons chia seeds
2 tablespoons brown sugar
2 tablespoons ground flax seed
2 tablespoons oat bran
1/8 teaspoon salt

Directions:
1. Heat a skillet over medium heat and add the pistachios. Toast for a few minutes, just until slightly golden and fragrant. Pour the pistachios into a large bowl.
2. Add the coconut to the same skillet over medium heat. Stir and shake the pan until the coconut is slightly toasted, about 2 to 3 minutes. Add the coconut to the bowl.
3. Add the oats, pineapple, wheat bran, chia seeds, sugar, flax seed, oat bran and salt to the bowl with the pistachios and coconut. Stir well to combine. Mix a few tablespoons with 1/2 or 1/3 cup plain greek yogurt and let it sit a few hours or overnight before eating.

Pumpkin & Honey Oats

Ingredients:
2 tablespoons almond butter
1/2 teaspoon vanilla extract
1/2 tablespoon maple syrup or honey
1/4 cup canned pumpkin not pumpkin pie filling
1/3 cup vanilla almond milk
1/2 cup old fashioned oats
1/4 teaspoon cinnamon
1/4 teaspoon pumpkin pie spice
Pinch of salt
2 tablespoons dark or milk chocolate chips

Directions:
1. In a small bowl, combine the almond butter, vanilla extract, and honey. Microwave for 10 seconds and then stir until well combined.
2. Add in the pumpkin, milk, and oats.
3. Stir well and make sure the almond butter is mashed in thoroughly.
4. Add in the cinnamon, pumpkin pie spice, and salt. Again stir well and then mix in the chocolate chips.
5. Transfer the mixture into a small jar or sealed container.
6. Place in the fridge for at least an hour or until oats are completely softened.

Figs and Nut Oats

Ingredients:

1/4 cup quick oats
1/2 cup almond milk
1/2 tablespoon chia seeds
1 fresh fig, sliced
1 tablespoon chopped pecans (or any nut)
1/2 tablespoon raw honey

Directions:

1. Place the oats, milk and chia seeds in a jar or a container with a lid; stir, cover and let it sit 1 to 2 hours, or refrigerate overnight.
2. Place in a bowl, top with figs, honey and chopped nuts.

Chocolate & Banana Oats

Ingredients:

1 small, ripe banana
2 tablespoons cacao powder
2 tablespoons sweetner (honey, coconut sugar, maple syrup), optional
2 tablespoons water
1/2 cup rolled oats
3 tablespoons chia seeds
1.5 cups full-fat coconut milk

Directions:

1. In a bowl, mash the banana with the cacao, sweetner if using, and water until it forms a smooth paste.
2. Stir in the oats and chia seeds, and then the milk, stirring continuously.
3. Place in the fridge overnight either in the bowl or in individual jars.
4. To serve it warm, add to a saucepan in the morning and heat over low to medium heat around 5 minutes. You may need to add some extra liquid at this point to thin a little if the porride is to thick.

Raspberry & Almond Oats

Ingredients:

1/2 cup rolled oats
1/2 coconut milk, plus a little extra
1/2 cup frozen raspberries
1 teaspoon chia seeds
3 teaspoons pure maple syrup
1 tablespoon sliced almonds

Directions:

1. Place rolled oats, coconut milk, raspberries, chia seeds, and 2 teaspoons maple syrup in a pint size mason jar container. Stir until everything is mixed together and oats are covered in liquid.
2. Place top on and store in the refrigerator overnight, 5-8 hours.
3. In the morning, stir in extra coconut milk to loosen up the oats up and to get the consistency you like.
4. Stir in almonds and serve.

Pecans & Cocoa Oats

Ingredients:

1/2 cup almond milk
1 medjool date, pitted and chopped
1/4 teaspoon pure vanilla extract
1/2 tablespoon cocoa powder
1/2 cup rolled oats
1-2 teaspoons maple syrup
2 teaspoons chopped pecans
sprinkle of sea salt

Directions:

1. In a pint size mason jar stir together almond milk, date, vanilla, and unsweetened cocoa powder until all combined.
2. Stir in rolled oats.
3. Place lid on and refrigerate for 8 hours or overnight.
4. Stir in a little extra almond milk to loosen oats up and to get the consistency you like.
5. Stir in maple syrup. Start with 1 teaspoon then give it a taste. If you need more sweetness then add in the rest.
6. Sprinkle with pecans and salt. Enjoy.

Peanut Butter & Banana Oats

Ingredients:

1/2 cup Banana Yogurt
1/3 cup rolled oats
1/3 cup almond milk
1 tablespoon peanut butter
1/2 banana sliced
handful of chocolate chips

Directions:

1. In a jar or bowl combine all ingredients together.
2. Cover the jar or bowl and place in the fridge overnight or for at least 4 hours.
3. Remove from fridge, get out your spoon, and go to town.

Peach & Nut Oats

Ingredients:

2 cups milk
1 cup dry old-fashioned oats
1 cup diced peaches in light syrup
2 tablespoons light brown sugar
1 tablespoon light butter spread
2 tablespoons honey
1/2 cup chopped walnuts or pecans
1/2 teaspoon cinnamon
1/4 teaspoon salt

Directions:

1. In a medium-sized mixing bowl, lightly mix all the ingredients together.
2. Spray the slow cooker with cooking spray. Pour oatmeal mixture into slow cooker and place lid on top. Set for low 4 hours.
3. The oats will be soft when finished.
4. To serve, pour milk over the top. Enjoy!

Chocolate & Chia Oats

Ingredients:

2 cups old fashioned oats
2 cups milk of your choice
1/4 cup cacao powder
1/4 cup pure maple syrup
3 tablespoons chia seds

Directions:

1. In a medium bowl, whisk all ingredients together until well combined.
2. Divide into smaller containers such as mason jars, cover and place in refrigerator overnight.
3. Top with fresh fruit and enjoy!

Walnut & Vanilla Oats

Ingredients:

1/2 cup rolled oats
1 tablespoon flax
1/2 cup water
2/3 cup vanilla yogurt
1 tablespoon brown sugar
1 tablespoon walnut pieces

Directions:

1. In the bottom of a mason jar or a container add oats and flax, then pour water over the oats, and cover with vanilla yogurt. No need to stir.
2. Refrigerate overnight (8-12 hours).
3. In the morning top with Brown Sugar and Walnut pieces and enjoy!

Banana & Cinnamon Oats

Ingredients:

1 cup rolled oats
1/2 banana, mashed
1/2 teaspoon cinnamon
1/2 teaspoon vanilla extract
1 tablespoon Maple Syrup
1 teaspoon flaxseed meal
3/4 cup milk

Directions:

1. In a medium-sized container, mash 1/2 banana.
2. Then, mix in the rest of ingredients and let soak for at least 2 hours or overnight.
3. Serve with coconut whipped cream, sliced banana, and a dash of cinnamon!

Blueberry & Nut Oats

Ingredients:
1/2 banana mashed
1/2 cup oats
1/4 cup almond milk
1 tablespoon chia seeds
1 tablespoon flaxseeds

Blueberry-cashew cream:
1/2 banana
1/2 cup blueberries
1 medjool date
2 tablespoons cashew nuts
4 tablespoons milk

Directions:

1. For the oat mixture, mix all ingredients together in a bowl, make sure the banana is mashed before you add it!
2. For the creamy topping add all ingredients to your blender and simply blend until totally smooth. add the oats to the bottom of a jar, or glass and top with the cream.
3. Leave in the fridge overnight and enjoy in the morning.

Pineapple & Vanilla Oats

Ingredients:

1/2 cup pineapples
1 tbsp coconut flakes
1/2 tsp vanilla extract
1/2 cup rolled oats
1/2 cup milk

Directions:

1. For extra fanciness: blend the pineapple together with the vanilla extract and coconut flakes.
2. Layer oats and milk and pineapple mash one after each other.
3. Leave in the fridge overnight and enjoy in the morning.

Blueberry & Lemon Oats

Ingredients:
1/2 cup rolled oats
1/2 cup milk
4 tbsp blueberries
1 tsp maple syrup
1 tsp lemon zest
2 tsp lemon juice
5 tbsp natural yogurt

Directions:

1. Mix all ingredients.
2. Place that mixture into a jar.
3. Leave in the fridge overnight and enjoy in the morning.
4. Enjoy!

Grape & Lemon Oats

Ingredients:

1/2 cup rolled oats
1/2 cup milk of choice
1 small handful grapes, sliced in half
2 tablespoons walnuts, crumbled
5 tablespoons natural yogurt
1/2 teaspoon cinnamon
1 teaspoon maple syrup

Directions:

1. Place all ingredients into a bowl and mix them well.
2. Place mixture into a jar. place it in the fridge.
3. Hold on for a couple of hours. Then enjoy.

Lime & Coconut Oats

Ingredients:
1/2 cup rolled oats
1/2 cup almond milk
1/2 cup plain Greek yogurt
2 teaspoons chia seeds
1 tablespoons coconut sugar
zest and juice of 1 large lime
1/4 teaspoon coconut extract
1/4 teaspoon vanilla extract

Directions:

1. Combine all of the ingredients in a bowl and stir together until well combined.
2. Cover the bowl and place in the fridge overnight to soak.
3. In the morning, fluff up the oats with your spoon and then dig in!

*If you want, sprinkle some toasted coconut on top or some local honey.

Printed in Great Britain
by Amazon